Plane Sh.

MW00333976

Robin Morris

A comprehensive and in-depth guide to making a surfboard.

All the tricks, shortcuts and secrets revealed.

With this book you will make a surfboard to be proud of.

Produced & Distributed By Assegai Publishing
e-mail: southwestjbay@truewan.co.za
PO Box 1588 Jeffreys Bay, 6330 South Africa
All Copyrights Reserved.
First Printed In December 2003.
Reproduction: Walker Ah Hing; Port Elizabeth
Printing: PEB Port Elizabeth

ASSEGAI
PUBLISHING
JEFFREYS BAY

www.assegaipublishing.com

With Thanks...

To: Thys Strydom, shaper extraordinaire and his able team -

Stephen van de Watt – the wizard spray artist ;

Norman – the lamination man;

Makriel – Mr Patience, for sanding and polishing;

and Christo – who does a bit of everything.

Thanx Guys!

Someone we all knew...

His name was *Jimi* and he lived in *Electric Ladyland*

Usually *Stone Free* he enjoyed *Castles Made Of Sand*

Met his *Foxy Lady* on the *Rainbow Bridge* with the *Voodoo Child*

Covered in *Purple Haze* from the *Spanish Castle Magic*

That dusted his *Gypsy Eyes*

Who Knows he had a *Machine Gun*

That let him stand next to the *Fire...*

Jimi says it was *The Burning Of The Midnight Lamp*

That flew him around *The Third Stone From The Sun*

But only on a full moon when *The Wind Cries Mary*

Can you still hear him whisper:

"Hey Joe, fly on *Little Wing...!"*

Contents

~ One ~

So you want to make a surfboard. Maybe you've surfed quite a lot already and know what it is that particularly works for you or maybe you've just started and decided to make your own board because it's part of the stoke of surfing.

Whatever, it doesn't matter. The intention with this guide is to try and make sure you follow the right process and make yourself the best surfboard possible.

Making surfboards is an art. Shapers are unique. Covered in foam dust all day, they emerge from their shaping bays with these incredibly flimsy shaped pieces of foam. Aerodynamic in every sense, each plug of foam is meticulously hand shaped into a missile of extreme beauty.

All the secrets gained over years of honing their craft go into every board. Each curve and hollow is processed with deft care to ensure that every board produced excels in performance, completely in tune with the magic of the ocean and her timeless energy.

Speed, stability, driving power-turns, its all there in the final shape. Not too much and not too little makes the difference. It's a science gained through trial and error and every shaper will tell you his war stories of how he started out and what his first shapes looked like. How he burned his first shaped plug by mixing the resin too hot with the hardener when he glassed it and so on. The stories are legend.

Well those guys never had this guide to follow when they started out like you have. So, hopefully we can remove a lot of the stigma and secrecy attached to the manufacture of surfboards and provide you with a hands-on guide of what to do and how to do it.

All the materials, all the tools you'll need, da worx!

If you give someone a set of brushes and some paints and ask them to paint a picture, they may not be able to create anything. It takes an artist, but if you give someone the tools and then also give them a *'paint by numbers'* picture, it's a lot easier.

Same analogy applies here.

The process that follows is not necessarily the law. Shapers from all over the world do some of the steps differently. Will even argue and contend some points and probably provide sufficient support for alternative methods that work better. They'll offer some valid shortcuts.

That's awesome...!

The intention here isn't to be contentious. This is not the bible of surfboard manufacture.

For this guide, I was privileged to work with legendary Jeffreys Bay shaper, **Thys Strydom**. To-date **Thys** has made in excess of six thousand surfboards. He surfs regularly at the world renowned right hand reef break, *'Super Tubes'* in Jeffreys Bay and still shapes and produces some of the finest surfboards the world has to offer from his factory – *'The Surfboard Factory'*.

This is a state of the art full production factory situated in Jeffreys Bay. The factory overlooks an awesome right-hander called *'Kitchen Windows'*. The view alone has to be an inspiration for any shaper. Thys provided all the technical background to make this guide possible. A lot of the surfing information came from talking to the pros and from creditable surf magazines like *'Zigzag'*.

To set the stage, surfboards come in all shapes and sizes so we're going to start by getting a little more familiar with the sport of surfing plus we'll go into some detail on surfboards in particular.

You basically get a different shaped board for every type of wave. For large waves you need a bigger board. For small waves the reverse. For fast down the line reef breaking waves you need a narrow board. For beach breaks, a wider board. This means you actually need a lot of different boards for all the different breaks.

Beware - Big quivers of boards cost big bucks!

The various classifications, the shapes, features and designs are all important. You need to take cognisance of all the aspects including your height, weight and surfing ability before you decide on your actual surfboard specifics.

Surfboards are loosely classified into the following:

Fish   Hybrid   Short Board   Mini Mal   Long Board   Gun

The Fish – this is a short wide board with a wide swallow tail. It's a high performance board, ideal for doing tricks and spins on small beach break type waves. It's a lot of fun. It's a little wider and thicker so it paddles well which means you can catch waves easily even though the board is shorter.

The Hybrid - This is really a larger Fish without the wide swallow tail and is more suited to your beginner to intermediate surfer. It has a lot more buoyancy, is longer, thicker and yet still very manoeuvrable. Suitable for most types of waves. It's a good all round board.

Conventional Short Board - This means a standard shaped board not more than 7'2" in length. A good surfer will have at least two boards. Normally a 6'3" or a 6'4" as his standard all wave board and then maybe a 6'8" or 6'10" going up to 7'2" for bigger waves.

Mini Mal - More suited to older surfers. This board starts at around 7'2" and goes up to about 8'0" in length. The board is notably wider, thicker and fuller in shape compared to a conventional short board.

The plus factor here is that for the older surfer this board provides all the stability and manoeuvrability without being too loose in a wave. It will also paddle well which gives the older surfer and even chance of catching as many waves as the young guns.

The ideal shape for a Mini-Mal is to match the tail width with the nose. A soft Pintail will work far better for down the line speed going into hard, driving turns off the top than a squash tail which will be a little restricting when going for a big carve on a longer board like this.

Picture the shape of a fisherman's spoon which is rounded on both ends but still retains a point. Same principle applies here for the ideal shape of a Mini-Mal. A well shaped, aerodynamic Mini-Mal can really perform. Will also move like a tank if not shaped correctly.

Long Board – Nowadays, used by surfers of all ages. More popular though with older surfers who prefer long boards, not only for nostalgic reasons but because the surfer is able to catch almost any wave due to the awesome paddling power it offers.

These boards start at about 9′0″ in length and go right up to 10′6″ with three stringers, and even added aesthetics like a wooden nose block and a wooden tail block. They are pieces of art and have an extremely loyal following.

On small wave days long boards are an incredible amount of fun because you can walk to the nose and do a whole bunch of tricks. There is even a pro long boarding world surfing circuit where the cream of the world's long boarders compete at various surf destinations around the world.

The pro surfer's long board is glassed super light and is ultra aerodynamic in shape. These guys throw their boards around in a wave like a short board.

Awesome to watch...!

Gun - This is purely a big wave board. Shaped like a bullet with a very sharp pintail, narrow width from rail to rail and quite thick. These boards are designed for speed on really big waves. Some of them have straps on the deck for surfers to strap their feet in, to prevent them from bouncing off the board on big waves.

Surfbreaks

Then of course you get a whole bunch of different breaks suitable for the above boards. Throughout the world the average coastline differs as it winds down the natural course and flow created from the land.

Each bay, each segment of coastline, each reef and every point is unique. This allows the ocean's massive wave patterns to break with God like supremacy on every coast, producing radically different sets of waves in size, power and shape.

Originating from the two Poles (North & South) or generated way out in the ocean from a monster storm, majestic waves are formed, producing massive peaks that travel infinite distances to every coastal destination. Surfers wait in anticipation for these sets of waves to arrive at their particular break.

Like magnets, they're drawn to the ocean's deliveries and get to ride the endless lines of perfection. There are never enough waves to satisfy a surfer.

Trippy stuff...

Kelly Slater enjoying some tube time at Super Tubes - Jeffreys Bay

This is what makes every surfer continually search for that next elusive wave, because no two waves are the same. A beach break will provide a short really fun wave with a few tubes and some radical snaps and turns.

Whereas a fast down the line reef break will surge the adrenalin to breaking point as the surfer searches for that intangible tube ride trying desperately to avoid getting crunched onto the merciless reef below where razor sharp coral awaits.

Then there's the big wave day. Just the paddle out takes nerves of steel. Even at six foot a powerful wave can hold a surfer down until his lungs are at bursting point.

Only to surface and take another one on the head...!

Or try free falling down the face of a big wave, hit the bottom and wait anxiously as the mighty ocean delivers a massive foam-ball on top of you with bone crushing force. The sound alone is like an express freight train running just above you.

Going Big At Mavericks...

Scares the bravest of men.

Requires big goonies...!

This is however all part of it. Adrenalin charged, constantly searching. Surfers don't refer to surfing as a sport. They call it a lifestyle because once you've been sucked in it's very difficult to let go.

Okay, let's go make a surfboard....!

~ Two ~

Previously, we looked at the different types of surfboards. In this chapter we're going to analyse the intrinsic shapes, features and designs of surfboards as we know them today.

Take careful note here because this may sound a bit confusing but it's necessary that you understand all the detail so that you'll know beforehand what type of board you ultimately want to make that's going to work best for you.

Boards are shaped for various waves and are therefore shaped in different sizes and dimensions. All aspects are very important for the final product, ideally suited to a surfer's weight, height and style of surfing.

Tail Designs

Tail designs offer many choices. This is the easiest area to determine because the designs are all so radically different but it is without doubt the most performance related factor. So, we'll begin with this area of design.

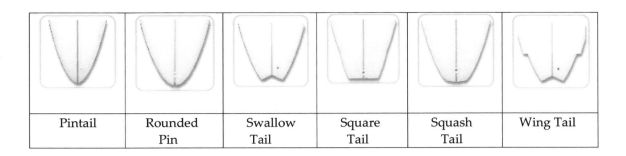

Pintail	Rounded Pin	Swallow Tail	Square Tail	Squash Tail	Wing Tail

Even a novice can see the difference in the various tail designs due to all the radically alternate shapes. However, each shape and feature is suitable for different wave conditions.

Basically, longer boards will respond better with rounder tails because of the smoother rail to rail spin whereas shorter boards will opt for performance and therefore favour Swallow, Wing or Squash tails.

Here are some of the more popular tail designs:

Pintail - meaning the tail comes to a narrow point. It will have less drive due to the reduced area. A narrow pin is ideally suited to big waves or perfect surf where drive isn't important. Fast down the line speed waves breaking on a shallow reef are where a Pintail and a Wing Tail excel.

Pintails are also good for conventional short boards over 6'6" in length and Mini-Mals. There are various types of Pintails. The narrower the pin the more gun it becomes, which means big waves and a lot of speed whereas the more rounded the pin the better it is for small waves.

Lots of fun, easy turns, more stable and a quicker response.

The narrower the pin, the higher up the board will be the widest point. We refer to this area as the *'Hip'* of a surfboard. Picture any kind of missile built for speed. It will have a narrow tail going into its widest point about two thirds of the way up the body and then tapering off into a point.

Similar scenario here.

Squash - Then you get the traditional Square and the Rounded Square known as a *'Squash Tail'* because it looks like the tail has been all squashed in. It's called traditional because it is the perfect all round design tail that works on all waves, providing a lot of drive with still a lot of freedom. Nice in small wave conditions and beach breaks when a lot of speed needs to be generated. Also very popular with long boards.

Swallow Tail - Similar in performance to a Squash Tail although it looks completely different as it resembles the tail of the swallow bird. Also used for generating speed, a Swallow Tail's response in changing direction is even faster than a Squash Tail because the water wraps around the tip of each swallow and locks the water in like a funnel. Good for tube riding and going around the lip of a wave where you need some hold. It will also dig in deep for strong power surfing.

Moving up the board we get to the *'Hip'* or the widest point as previously mentioned. This alters the design of the tail as well. The *'Hip'* of a board pulls the tail area in, enhancing maximum water flow along the rails.

The narrower the board the faster it will fly whereas the wider the board the more displacement of water to work with but the board will be that much more stable and easier to ride.

This leads us onto the rails. A lot of surfers say the rails are not that important unless you're a very good surfer. Good surfers, the kind who literally dig their rails in deep on almost every turn, are going to want to focus on very specific rail designs.

Low   Medium   Full

The rail helps in a lot of areas. Its main function is to disperse water along the flow. There are only a few choices. Each design or feature works a little differently.

- A medium or soft rail - will cut easily through the face of a wave.
- A full or boxy rail - will be harder to bury but can also pop out of the wave if not controlled. It will however provide a lot of drive.
- A lower or pinched rail – it will bury very easily and won't pop out which is good for doing hard carves and power turns.

The bottom rail starts at the tail with a sharp edge going up the rail into a nice rounded 'C' shape at the middle and then tapers off into a very soft 'C' shape up the board. The sharper the edge of the rail, the more the board will have both grip and drive.

Too much grip can cause the board to catch or dig in on the face of the wave. Not enough edge will cause the board to have insufficient drive because the rail won't grip the water's surface.

Driving Hard Off The Top...

The format of the rail depends mainly on needs like weight,

and the surfers' ability, so a shaper will always take extra care in determining how much of the top deck to roll from the stringer to the rail. This is from the centre stringer to the outer rail edge.

Low or pinched rails are ideal for fast waves and the more experienced surfer. Medium or soft rails are good for all round conditions as they are the most forgiving. Boxy/full rails are more suited to beginners and small wave conditions.

The rails will of course also be determined by the thickness of the board. Beginner surfers will usually require a thicker board. Obviously, a thicker board is also going to be better for a heavier surfer.

Anything from 2 ¾ inches to 3.0 inches will provide a nice stable board that is easy to paddle, enabling the surfer to catch waves without cliff-hanger late takeoffs to contend with. More experienced surfers will go for a thickness of about 2.5 inches for an average conventional high performance short board.

The Pro's want their boards ultra light so they start at around 2.2 inches but a board this thin isn't going to last very long. A couple of big floaters and the pressures that emerge will soon weaken the board enough for it to crease across the deck or even snap in two.

Big bucks wasted...!

Possibly the most intriguing shaping feature is the bottom. It's also the most contentious when it comes to a lot of shaper's personal points of view.

Theoretically, what happens is that water flows from the top of the board down, creating friction, which causes drag on the bottom of the board at the point of contact.

Obviously this energy release can be used to the surfer's advantage if channelled off correctly. As the water flows down the board it speeds up and then hits the tail area where there is some drag. When the surfer does a snap turn, the board reacts and the water flow changes direction across the bottom of the board creating a whole new water flow and energy release.

It is necessary then to understand that the water direction is almost like a hydro-plane which radically alters a board's response wherever the bottom of the board comes into contact with the water flow.

Result: shapers have created a range of bottom designs to cater for individual surfer's needs.

The basic flat bottom was popular long ago. Water wasn't dispersed to the maximum advantage but it was ideal for speed although it offered limited manoeuvrability. Shapers soon advanced to the more traditional bottom shapes that are popular today.

The Vee bottom (or convex bottom) is probably the most popular as it is the easiest to surf. Think of the basic shape of the bottom of most ships. They have an enhanced Vee bottom.

A surfboard with a slight Vee will be enough to force the water away from the centre of the board in a cutting motion that disperses the water evenly down the bottom of the board. This shape makes the board stable and easy to turn and will get the board onto its rail a lot faster.

This feature is ideally suited to wider boards.

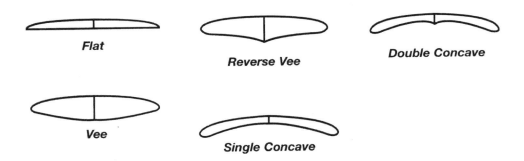

The Concave bottom adds another whole dimension. You get single and double Concaves. A single would be across the entire board whereas the double Concave is from the outer rail to the centre stringer and then repeated from the stringer to the outer rail so that if you hold the board up to your chest and look down towards the tail you'll see two distinctive concaves identical in shape going from each outer rail to the centre stringer.

Concaves are quite unique as they offer both lift and speed and maximize the hydro-plane effect. This will also offer a lot of drive in hard turns as the concaves allow the water to flow through the centre while still applying pressure on the rails.

This offers support down the line of the board. Concaves are good for open face waves, lots of speed and driving turns. They are very popular with a lot of surfers. Good for narrow boards.

A channel bottom is a series of channels that transverse from the tail up the board, gently fading out completely before the halfway point. Channels offer a lot of grip as the water disperses over and then through the channels locking in like a mini vacuum. Very good for fast down the line type waves, reef breaks and radical point breaks.

The ideal for the average surfer would be to go for a combination of both a slight Vee and a concave.

Result - most boards' will feature a combination of a flatter bottom up front blending into a concave through the middle and then flowing into a Vee through to the tail. The trick here is to ensure that it all fits in with the overall flow of the shape of the board.

This brings us to the rocker or curve of a board which can also have a big impact on a board's performance. A board with a lot of rocker or curve through the board is ideally suited to fast hollow waves but will lack speed on open flatter waves.

Associated with the overall design of the bottom deck, the curve or rocker is divided into four main areas.

First there is the nose kick. This prevents the board from nose diving on take off or dipping in the face of a wave. Too much curve will create difficulty in paddling into a wave.

Really not fun in strong off-shore wind conditions.

Second is the curve through the middle section which is all about the paddling effectiveness of the board and the overall speed of the board. This is where the board comes into contact with the water. Shapers will want to restrict the curve here a little without affecting the flow of the overall shape of the board.

Third is the area in front of the fins. This is where the water flow drags a bit before it hits the tail area. The curve will adjust here in relation to the middle and tail curve sections.

Finally, the tail curve area. Too much and the board will drag. Too little and you'll lose the drive which is so important in the tail area. Too much of any of the above and the board will lack speed and too little will have the opposite effect.

You need the nose kick and then a slight rocker going almost flat for the trimming area where the water makes contact with the board providing the speed and drive. You then need a good bottom curve strategically shaped down the board to make the board as manoeuvrable as possible.

The balance is all about aerodynamics. This means getting that bottom shape to flow from tip to tail. An experienced eye can look down a board and immediately spot where the imperfections are.

It should run in one even line, both sides identical from outer rail to centre stringer, from the nose curve down through the middle and out though the tail.

This is why good shapers' are called artists...!

There are some other concaves like Spoon Noses and Bonzo concaves which some surfers prefer to have on their boards. Be careful with these because the deeper the concave the more drag it creates, which reduces speed.

Long boarders will often go for a Spoon Nose which is a deep concave shaped like a spoon in the nose of the board to allow the surfer a hydro effect when nose riding on a full nosed long board. This means a long board with a nose design that is almost the same width as the middle section of the board.

On small wave days, this can be so much fun because a long board traditionally paddles well anyway due to its length so the Spoon Nose doesn't really hamper the speed aspect.

Surfers can then walk to the nose and stand with both feet on the nose of the board without the nose dipping on the face of a wave. In competitions this move scores high points. It also provides a fun surf day.

The Bonzo concave is situated under the tail. It's a slight concave that runs from the tail area up the bottom of the board about a third of the way. Once again this aids water flow through and out the tail area. Normally, the water catches in this area meeting the resistance of the fins. The Bonzo helps to overcome this drag.

Taking the overall basic shape of your board into consideration, the best option is to break the basic outline down into three parts.

Namely – the Nose; the Hip; and the Tail.

The most common size breakdown for the three parts, taking your average 6'4" board is as follows:

- The Nose – 11 inches
- The Widest point (the Hip) – 18.5 inches
- The Tail – 14 inches

Using this scale you can mark out any conventional surfboard according to the length. Remember, the surfer's weight and height are also very important factors when determining the length, width and how thick the board has to be.

Fins

We now get to an area that is without doubt the most controversial subject. From the pros to your average surfer, everyone is an authority on fins. It is the one area of development that has really progressed.

In days gone by in Hawaii and Polynesia they rode boards without fins. It was only in 1950 when American Tom Blake started using a fin on his woody that everyone got interested. Tom Blake came up with the concept after watching yachts using an aft fin for turning.

The single fin improved with time as did surfboards. Wooden boards and fins were replaced with foam cores strengthened with glass fibre and resin.

Fin designs changed as well. Larger fins for big waves. More rake, better foiling. They got lighter and more flexible. Then came the removable box fins.

It was all happening.

Enter Mark Richards. An Aussie Pro surfer who decided that two fins would optimally be better than one. And he was so right. Richards launched his Twin Fin on the world surfing arena. Two identical fins placed apart.

Richards literally shredded small waves from top to bottom in a new style of surfing on his Twin Fin and it instantly caught on worldwide. Overnight, boards went shorter and wider and the race was on to be the most radical surfer in the water.

The difference now was that surfing suddenly took on a creative new dimension. The old single fin that drove hard off the bottom stylised a soulful way of surfing. With a Twin Fin, surfers went vertical off the lip.

A whole new style of surfing followed.

Radical & Freestyle...

Contest surfing rules had to be changed. Richards went on to win four consecutive world surfing titles stamping his authority on competitive surfing. The double finned surfboard ruled.

Not for long though. Aussie surfer of note, a big guy named Simon Anderson, introduced yet another fin onto the twin fin. Looking for a bit more stability to handle his large frame, he found the twins to be a little too loose so he placed a centre fin further back.

Anderson quietly introduced his three-fin *'Thruster'* to the surfing world, little realizing what a massive impact it would have. The *'Thruster'* is still the standard fin structure today. Extremely responsive and reliable, the three fin triangle placement works in all surf conditions.

The sad thing is that Anderson failed to copyright his design. Millions of surfers use his system everyday for free. Anderson's had to put it all down to the development of surfing. He has however earned his stripes and his name will always be associated with his innovation.

The other major development since Anderson's input has been the removable fin systems. This has allowed surfers the freedom to remove their fins when travelling or to be able to choose a different fin set for different waves without having to change surfboards.

For travelling, removable fins can be safely packed away and then screwed in when required, which saves a lot of frustration to a surfer who is far away from home and unzips his board bag on arriving at his destination only to find that during travel one or more of the fixed fins have snapped off his board, rendering it useless.

Big problem...!

There are some very good companies who have made huge strides in producing the ultimate removable fin for most surf conditions. FCS designed a range of fins for every requirement that allows the surfer to carry an assortment of fin packs. This enables the surfer to select the fins most suitable for the surf's conditions.

FCS fins fit flush with the bottom curve of the board and react as well as any fixed fin. They're that good but nothing still beats a fixed fin for the real thing especially when you're looking at some serious big surf and you really need those fins to work for you.

Removable Fins

The reason for fins is to give the board stability and turning power. Turning on a board by leaning hard into a wave creates pressure on the fins from the water and bends them slightly until the fin snaps back providing the drive which is that adrenaline pumped feeling one gets when going hard off the bottom of a wave. The bigger the fin, the more drive but also the more drag in the water.

You need both speed and drive. You want a fin to dig deep on a large wave but you also need the speed of the board to get around the wave. The pros today mostly opt for a smaller set of fins because speed is everything. They rely on their incredible skill and speed and the board's rails to hold the turns.

The actual fin shape then has become quite scientific. Shapers and specialized fin manufacturers look at the following main areas:

- The Base
- The Depth
- The Foil
- The Rake
- The Flex
- The Splay
- The Tow

The Standard Fin...

The Base - the wider the base the stiffer the performance of the board but it will also enhance the drive. Too wide will be too restricting, whereas too thin will be too slippery.

The Depth - a deep fin will provide a lot of hold on turns and will be good for big waves. Less depth has the opposite effect but will work in small waves.

The Foil - the central fin is foiled on both sides whereas the side fins are foiled on one side only. Hold the board with the tail on the ground with the nose up towards your chest. Look down the flow of the board and you'll clearly see the foil on the fins. The side fins will be foiled on the outside only, closest to the rail. A surfboard will always turn towards the foil. This is accentuated when the surfer leans onto the rail. The more a fin is foiled the better the board will turn.

The Rake - the more raked back the fin, the more drawn out the turn. Ideal for big waves or fast down the line type surfing. Whereas the more upright the fin shape is, the tighter the turning circle becomes. Ideal for small waves and performing tricks, 360's, aerials, etc.

The Flex - the stiffer the fin, the more responsive. Using your thumb, bend the tip of the fin and test how snappy it returns. A stiff fin is perfect for speed whereas more flexible fins are better suited to slower manoeuvres where you need to spread the load through a turn.

It doesn't all stop here because you still have to decide on the position where you're going to place the actual fins on the bottom of the board. This is very important and relies on two aspects:

- Splay
- Tow

The Splay - this is the angle of the two side fins. The ideal is to splay the fins out by 5 degrees. Definitely not more than 10 degrees. The wider the splay (10 degrees) the better the board is for small waves. For larger surf a lesser splay is required. Big guns for monster waves will be splayed as little as 2 degrees.

The Tow - the outside fins are towed inwards and should ideally point slightly towards the nose. This is the standard. Too much tow will slow the board down. Fins that are set inwards will generate speed into and out of turns whereas fins that are set in more of a straight line will be good for speed on down the line type waves.

Placing the two outside fins closer to the rail will loosen the board up. Moving the side fins back and the centre fin forward will provide the board with a tighter turning circle.

The complexities of shaping as you can now see are endless. It's a sort of combination of the true artist and the scientific approach to water dynamics and how this impacts on the surfer's ability to maximise each wave.

Each surfer is unique although all surfers will try and emulate the Pros which is difficult to do by any means because they have always set the standards. It's very confusing and all comes down to trial and error and personal choice at the end of the day. It's what ultimately works best for you.

Now you have a good overall idea of what design is all about and you're probably totally confused but don't be. The fun has just begun. The concept of learning about design is essential for the shaper to create a surfboard that is ultimately going to work.

New surfboards cost a lot of money so you want to make sure that before you begin shaping your masterpiece you have a very good idea upfront of what you want to achieve.

Plan your masterpiece carefully down to the last detail. Take careful note of everything we've discussed here and have your requirements and design carefully mapped out and planned before you start.

What we're going to get into next is a general discussion on the kind of premises you will need to handle the entire process.

Just Another Day At The Office...!

~ Three ~

To begin our mission you need to have the right premises. The layout for an average surfboard factory requires the following:

- a shaping bay
- a spray booth
- a laminating area
- a sanding room
- and a polishing room.

This is the magic process a board goes through from beginning to end.

First, the foam plug gets shaped. Next, the board moves to the spray booth for the spray design. The board then gets laminated with glass fibre and resin before moving to the sanding bay. Finally, the polishing and finishing touches are applied.

You may not have access to all this amount of space. Probably only have a double garage, maybe even less space. If so, then you are going to do a lot more work as you will have to prepare the room for each stage.

Making surfboards is a messy business. It gives off a lot of pollution. Plus, there are times when you are going to need a clinically clean room like for spraying a design onto the foam.

At Home In The Shaping Bay...

For the shaping bay you will need a complete room at least four metres by four metres in size. You'll also need two trestles to place the board on. Trestles are best made of iron or steel and must be firmly bolted to the floor.

If you don't bolt the trestles to the floor then you need to sink the trestles into barrels or buckets filled with concrete. It's important that the trestles are very stable.

The trestle should form the shape of a 'T' and ideally be about navel height. It will differ for each shaper in order to accommodate his/her back. Shapers are known to suffer from back and hip problems in later life.

The centre of the trestles across the 'T' needs to be 'U' shaped. This is the yoke. It is necessary because when shaping and sanding the rails of a board, the board will lie in the yoke of the trestle exposing the rail. The entire top section of the trestle must be wrapped in foam rubber and masking tape to ensure adequate protection for the board.

Hand Made Trestles

You then need fluorescent lighting. This is very important! Lighting needs to be exceptionally good. You need a row of double fluorescents placed on either side of the room, mounted on the wall. The height of the lights from the floor must be just above the foam blank when the blank is lying on the trestles.

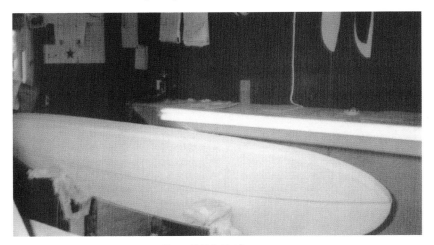

Good Lighting...

You'll also need an adequate plug point for your skill Planer's electricity supply. Make sure you have a lead extension from the plug point to your planer so that your planer has sufficient freedom to move without restriction.

A set of headphones to soften the noise of your planer and a good face mask to protect you from the foam dust are also necessary. You may start to resemble a creature from Mars but the protection is worth it in the long term.

Then we get the spray booth. This needs to be a completely closed in area or room with a set of trestles and good overhead fluorescent lighting. You will also need a set of wall mounted surfboard racks, mounted on the wall.

Spray Booth...

This is to store the finished spray designs and to store the freshly shaped blanks. At this stage it is critical that dust and dirty areas are avoided. The blanks need to be kept clinically clean until they have been laminated.

Use a pair of latex gloves to handle the boards. You must not get fingerprints on the freshly shaped blank as it is very difficult to remove them. This is an annoying problem that is often overlooked.

You will also need a plug point for your compressor. The compressor is necessary to power your spray gun as nearly all the design work is done in airbrush format. A really good facemask is vital as the fumes from the paints and thinners are extremely toxic.

We now move into the lamination area. This can be quite a large open room with a few sets of trestles depending on how much work you have. You need more than one set of trestles because when you've done the one side of a board you need to let it dry, which means you can then work on another board on another set of trestles, without restricting your work flow.

 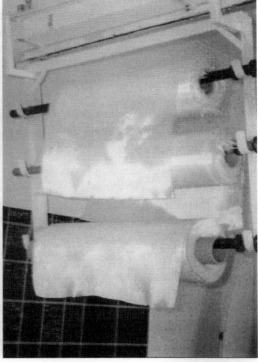

Laminating Area   **Overhead Cloth Reel Feeder**

You'll need surfboard wall racks mounted on the wall to hold the boards for work in progress.

Wall racks are best done in steel and should ideally consist of a frame with steel rods protruding out with about a metre distance between the rods. The rods can then be covered in rubber or foam or tape. This is to protect the boards when you store them on the racks.

In order to run the glass fibre cloth evenly over the board it's nice to have an overhead reel feeder for the cloth. This is a steel frame that has a small cylindrical reel attached to the frame almost like an enlarged toilet roll holder.

The roll of cloth is then put onto the cylinder and pulled off as desired straight onto the shaped foam nestling on the trestles.

Good overhead fluorescent lighting is important as is a heater if you're in a cold climate because the resin will not set if it drops below a certain temperature. Resin needs to be maintained at around room temperature for perfect conditions.

For the floor it is best to throw down cardboard to cover the entire floor. This can be changed as required and fresh cardboard brought in. The reason is that the resin dripping off the boards will destroy any naked floor area. So for protection, it is necessary to cover the floor area with a good strong cardboard.

Very important in this area is to have a large extraction fan. You will be working with toxic chemicals here. It is vital that an adequate face mask is used at all times and that the extraction fan is in good working order.

The external side of the extraction fan needs to be ducted into a filter system. This system can consist of sacking which can then be water flushed out daily with a strong hose.

You will also need a nice flat tabletop area where you'll do all your resin and hardener mixing and cutting of cloth for the fins and patching jobs. Drums of resin can also be stored underneath the table.

You will also need a plug point for the heater.

We now move into the sanding area.

This is an incredibly messy area with dangerous levels of very toxic dust. The room should be four metres square, big enough to accommodate a set of trestles that you can easily work around. The door of the room needs to be kept closed while sanding is being done to contain the dust.

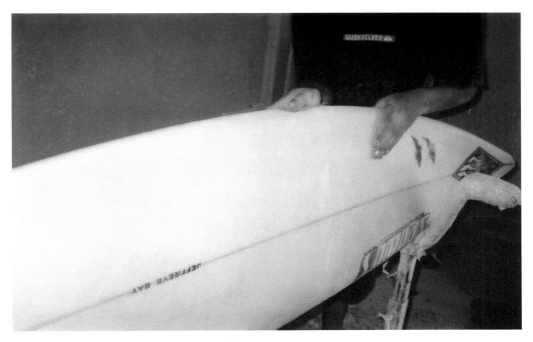

Sanding Room...

The lighting requirements are the same as in the shaping bay. Wall mounted double fluorescents, mounted on the wall just above the level of the surfboard when it is on the trestles. The sander needs good lighting to constantly check his work.

A plug point and extension lead is necessary for the operator to be able to move the hand held power sanding machine around without restriction. A large and very effective extractor fan is essential to suck out all the dust.

A face mask must be worn permanently while in this room. The external side of the extractor fan needs to be ducted into a similar sacking filter system like the laminating area and washed out daily.

The floor should ideally be bare concrete. This makes it easier to vacuum the floor at the end of every day to get rid of all dust particles. All the room's walls should ideally be painted white as white walls give off the best light reflection.

Most Municipalities will send Health Inspectors to inspect the laminating and the sanding bay area's periodically to ensure the toxic fumes are correctly exhausted. If these fumes and dust particles are allowed to freely permeate the surrounding air then it is a definite health hazard for everybody including animals within the near vicinity.

Finally, we get the Polishing Bay. This needs to be a standard room with a set of trestles and overhead fluorescent lighting. You'll need a plug point for the hand held polisher and an extension lead. The floor needs to be covered in cardboard as this can get quite messy.

Next, we'll have a look at all the tools and materials you'll need to have available prior to starting.

Focus...Focus...Focus...!

- Four -

There are not a lot of tools required to make a surfboard. You will need the basic big three hand held power tools like a variable speed Sander and Polisher, a Router and a Planer. These standard tools should last a long time if looked after properly. Buy established brand names and avoid disappointment in the long term.

You'll also need a set of basic tools:
- a sharp hand held flexible saw
- a steel rule
- a wood gauge
- a layout square or set square for accurately marking out fin and rail measurements
- a layout ruler which is a standard rule with a triangle head positioned in the middle of the ruler. Used for marking out accurate measurements off the centre as the triangle point lines up on the stringer, allowing the shaper to accurately measure from the centre to each outer rail
- a large pair of wooden callipers
- shaping blocks for sanding

- durable backing pads for sanding
- a spoke-shave for trimming the centre stringer
- a Stanley knife or scalpel
- a large scissors for cutting cloth
- a soft measuring tape – at least three metres
- a soft brush
- a three metre wooden dowel or straight edge
- a Surform which is a flexible blade type rasp/file used in conjunction with the shaping blocks for smoothing off the shaped areas of planed foam
- a mixed assortment of abrasive disks for the backing pads
- and a mixed assortment of grit sanding paper and water paper.

For the sandpaper you will need: 400 grit, 320 grit, 220 grit, 120grit and 80grit. For the water-paper you will need: 200 dry, 320 dry, 400dry, 600wet, 800 wet and 1 000 wet.

You'll need loads of it!

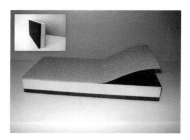

Sanding Block

Layout Rule

Surform

Rail Callipers

For spray work, you'll need at least a 100 horsepower compressor and a spray gun with two nozzles. One standard and one fine. This is for airbrushing artwork in the spray booth.

You will also use the compressor to blow off the foam dust that literally covers you from head to toe when you're busy shaping. Make sure your compressor has a long hose – at least twenty metres.

There are a variety of other little tools that you will need like a squeegee for laminating, small plastic trays for holding resin, a hard bristle broom for cleaning up, and an assortment of soft painting brushes which will also be used for cleaning up dust off blanks, etc.

That is about it for all the tools you will need. Look after them and you will get good use out of them. The materials you'll need are also fairly basic.

Blanks...

First, you'll need a blank. A blank is the actual foam. Correctly termed, *'High Density Polyurethane Foam'*. Also known by shapers as a *'plug'*. It will be supplied from the blank manufacturer with a centre stringer and a little kick in the nose.

Blanks are available in various sizes starting at around 6'0" right up to 10'6". Make sure you order the right size blank for the board you are shaping. Always order a blank that is at least two inches longer than the board you intend making.

You can also order custom made wooden tail blocks and nose blocks if you intend making a long board. This not only protects the board but adds to the aesthetics.

You'll need resin and hardener. For the resin, order laminating resin and sanding resin or filler resin as it is known in some countries. This is resin that contains Waxol. You will also need finishing resin which is a clear resin. The hardener is the catalyst that makes the resin set. The supplier will give you instructions on the mixing ratio for resin versus hardener.

Make sure you adhere to these instructions. Many a masterpiece has been completely destroyed by mixing the resin and hardener incorrectly. It's also dangerous as too much hardener will actually ignite. These chemicals are highly inflammable.

Beware...!

For glass fibre you will need both 6oz and 4oz cloth. Glass fibre is supplied on a roll. For super light glassing, use a layer of 4oz cloth on the top deck as well as on the bottom with a 4oz tail patch. The tail patch is normally about half a metre long.

For a normal or average laminating job you'll need a 4oz layer and 6oz layer of cloth on the deck plus a 6oz layer of cloth on the bottom for boards up to 6'6" in length.

For boards that are over 6'6" in length use a 6oz layer on the bottom and two layers of 6oz cloth on the deck. From this, one can determine how much cloth is necessary depending on the length of the surfboard.

As an average, for a standard 6'4" board, you will need:
- eight metres of glass fibre
- two litres laminating resin

- one litre sanding/filler resin
- one litre finishing resin
- 250ml catalyst
- four litres of Acetone

You will also need glass fibre *'Roving'* for the fins. These are strips of wound glass fibre that are used for building up the fins at the base to secure them in place. You'll be able to order this from the glass fibre supplier.

Roving...

Then you'll need:

- A standard leash plug
- A set of tri-fins
- At least a drum of Acetone for washing all the tools.
- A few rolls of adhesive masking tape
- Some 1 500 and 3 000 density rubbing compound motor vehicle polish
- Assorted acrylic paints
- Thinners for the spray artwork.

Note: only use acrylic paints for spray work on surfboards.

Okay, now you have it all.

Store the materials properly according to the directions provided by the respective suppliers.

Keep the blanks out of direct sunlight and all the chemicals and paints at room temperature.

Let's go and shape a surfboard...!

A Little Bit Of J/Bay Magic...Just To Inspire You...

~ Five ~

Now that we've discussed all the tools and the materials required, we can begin with the actual shaping process. First, ensure that you select the right size raw foam plug from the foam supplier.

Foam is actually made up of minute cells. This is a chemical compound that rapidly expands when mixed with a catalyst, evolving into tiny foam cells.

Foam suppliers blow their own blanks. This is done by pouring a small mix of the liquid chemicals into specially designed moulds. The chemicals quickly expand due to the catalyst, creating an enormous amount of pressure that condenses the micro foam cells to pinpoint size, thus ensuring a firm but still slightly flexible foam blank.

This is a highly technical process, done by specialised companies. The moulds have to be able to withstand enormous pressure and are therefore manufactured under strict controls and regulations.

The finished blank is then surgically split down the centre and a wooden quarter inch stringer (average) is glued to both centre sides and re-joined. The blank is then supplied complete with the centre wooden stringer. The stringer adds strength to the flimsy blank.

Now that you have your blank, lay it down deck side up on the trestles and have all your shaping tools ready.

Taking cognisance of all the data and options we discussed in previous chapters, you should have by now decided on the actual shape you want your board to be. This will include the tail design, bottom deck features, rails and the overall rocker required.

To begin, mark out the length of the board on the blank in pencil. Next, mark your nose, tail and widest point measurements onto the foam. Keep the measurements for the nose and tail positions at approximately twelve inches from either end of the blank.

Marking Out A Blank...

Using your layout rule with the triangle head placed on the centre stringer, pencil in points every twelve inches across the board that line up with the nose, tail and widest point marks that you made up and down the board.

Picture the paint by numbers concept.

Marry all your pencil points up and down the board and draw an initial outline of the board shape from rail to rail on the blank, including the tail design. If you have templates, then the job is a lot easier.

To make templates you ideally need a thin Perspex sheet that you can place over an existing board. Measure from the stringer to the rail, from about halfway down the board, all the way up to the nose. Draw the outline of the surfboard's shape on the actual Perspex. Using a jigsaw, cut out the shape on the Perspex and file the edges until smooth.

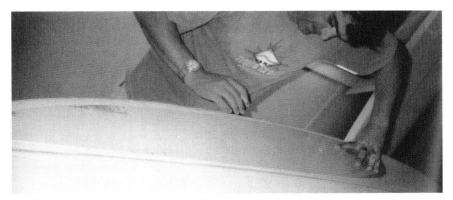

Using Templates...

To use a template, lay the template down on the foam blank with the straight edge on the centre stringer and pencil in the one half of the board's shape. Flip the template over to the other side of the stringer and pencil in the other half. Check your measurements with the layout rule.

Once you've completed pencilling in your basic shape on the foam plug, use the layout ruler with the triangle head again. Place the point of the triangle tip on the stringer and run the rule down the length of the board to ensure the rails are equidistant from the stringer down the whole board.

If you're happy, use a general-purpose flexible handsaw to cut out the design. Make sure you cut 2mm on the outside of the pencil line and that you keep the saw at ninety degrees to ensure the cut is transferred accurately all the way through.

Cutting Out The Blank...

Clean up the blank using the Surform. This will take off the rough foam edges.

This brings us to the rocker. To measure your rocker, you need a long flat wooden dowel that can serve as a straight edge. Turn the board over with the deck facing down and lay the dowel along the entire length of the bottom of the blank across the flat area.

Measuring The Rocker...

Measure both the tail and nose areas from the dowel down onto the blank and mark your rocker measurements on the tail, nose and widest point on the rails of the blank. Use the wood gauge to draw a pencil line down the length of the rails.

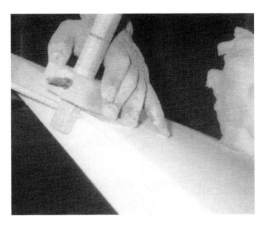

Using the Wood Gauge To Draw The Pencil Line...

Take into consideration how thick you want your board to be when establishing your rocker requirements. This will indicate to you how much of the blank you can shave.

You can now start planning in the bottom curve. Begin with the nose and work down towards the tail using long even strokes down the centre of the board working outwards to each rail.

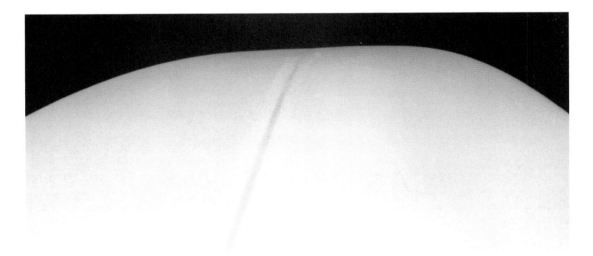

The Bottom Curve – Note The Single Concave...

Remember to ensure you have sufficient kick in the nose. Work down from the nose into your flat area and out through the tail. Use the Spoke-Shave to plane down the stringer. Using your planer for this will blunt the blade.

Holding the nose, tilt the board up towards your chest. Check down the length of the board to ensure your rocker runs as you intended. This is why you need good lighting.

Remember, you can always shave some foam off but you can never add it back on. When you've made your decision, stick to it.

Once you're happy with the bottom curve, clean up with the hand Surform to ensure you remove all the bumps and nicks.

Cleaning Up...

You can now plane in the feature on the bottom using your hand planer. This is the Vee or concave or whatever feature you've chosen. Try not to do any concaves on boards over 6'6" in length. Preferably use only Vee bottoms.

Take time on your feature to ensure that both sides of the Vee off the stringer are identical. The same with the concaves. If you are doing a single concave then it's a lot easier but if you are doing a double concave then both concaves must be identical from the rail to the stringer and vice versa. Variances here will obviously affect the overall performance of the board.

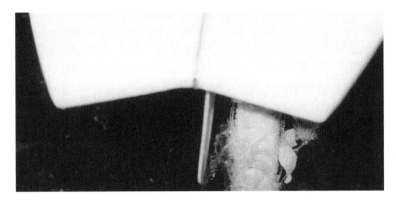

Planning In The Tail Feature...

You can now start on your tail feature. You will have chosen your tail design beforehand and made the necessary cuts with the hand saw when you first cut out the blank so your job here now is to ensure that the feature is enhanced and the rocker maintained.

Using the Surform plane in the tail feature taking care to ensure that the outer rails are identical and they follow through.

Once completed, clean up with a sand-block using 80 to 600 grit sandpaper until you get a nice smooth finish.

Okay, we're cooking...!

You're going to turn the bottom rail. Lay the board in the yoke of the trestles so that the rail is exposed to you. Use the wood gauge to draw a line in pencil down the blank fifteen centimetres from the outer rail going inwards and draw another line ten centimetres deep on the rail. These measurements will obviously depend on the size of the blank.

These are your lines.

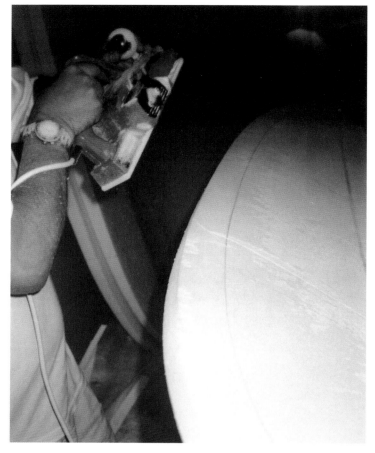

Planning The Rails...

Using the hand planer shave along the rail following the pencil lines. Concentrate on getting an even flow from the nose to the tail. The top rail is the important one. This is the bottom rail.

Get a nice rounded turn going up the board by taking off clean shaves along the entire length of the rail. Work from the middle up to the nose and then down towards the tail. Clean up using the sand-block with 80grit paper.

In the tail area you'll need a hard 90 degree edge which ideally continues to run just past the fin area up the rail and then fades off into a nice soft 'C' shape for the remainder of the bottom rail into the nose. You may well however have chosen a specific design for your bottom rail based on what we discussed in the previous chapters.

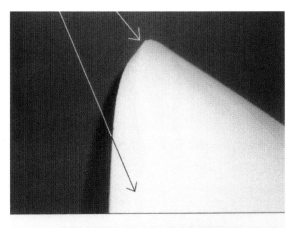

Bottom Rail - Tail Area
Note: The Straight Edge going into a Soft 'C'

Turn the board over to start on the deck. Your board is now beginning to take shape. Take a complete cut off the deck using the hand planer and continue to do so until the blank is down to the required thickness e.g. 2 ½ inches, of your choice.

Work from the centre of the board moving out towards the rails using long even strokes.

Use the big wooden callipers to constantly check the thickness of the rails and make sure both sides from the centre stringer to the rail are identical.

You are now going to take out all the excess foam in the nose with the Surform to highlight the kick. The foam at this stage will be very thin which means it can snap easily. Work carefully from the point in the nose back down into the meat of the board without altering the design of the nose.

Switch to the tail section and carefully remove all the excess foam from around your feature. The blank will be thin here now as well so work very carefully. Use a sand-block with 80grit paper to clean up until a smooth finish is achieved.

The entire blank must now be foiled from nose to tail. Use the Surform to remove any unwanted bumps, foam, nicks, etc. Make sure all your features like concaves, Vee's etc., are as you want them to be. Use a level to check that your deck is flat. Do any corrections wherever necessary.

We're going to start on the top rails. You will have pre-decided what type of rails you want on your board so we're going to use a standard rail design here for practicality.

Place the semi-shaped blank in the yoke of the trestle so that the one rail is directly exposed. For an average rail on a short board up to 6'6" in length you can cut 6cm in from the outer rail towards the stringer in the widest section of the board.

A Directly Exposed Rail Is easy To Work On...

Mark these measurements along the rail in pencil using the wood gauge. Ensure you run the gauge parallel to the rail edge in order to get a consistent pencil line down the length of the board.

For longer boards and Mini Mals, Mals, etc., you need to cut in 7cm. These measurements will reduce accordingly as you work towards the tail and then up towards the nose of the board.

You are now going to do the depth of the cut. For an average board, mark out 3cm from the top deck of the blank towards the middle of the blank. For a Mini Mal mark out 3.5cm and for a Mal mark out 4cm. Use the wood gauge to pencil in the lines.

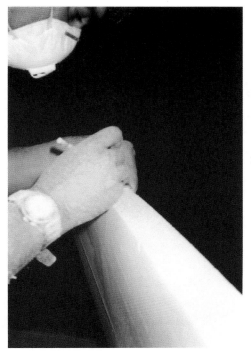

Mark In Pencil...

Using the hand plane, start in the centre of the board and gently remove entire cuts of foam along the length of the outer rails. Use long strokes across the length of the rail until you've arrived at the required measurement. Follow the pencil lines accurately.

Mowing The Rails...

The rail will now have a semi sharp edge on top going into a soft 'C' turned bottom rail. Using the sand-block gently taper the rails from the top into the bottom. Start from the middle of the board and work down towards the tail and then up towards the nose. The rails must flow along the length of the entire board.

Getting There...!

You should end up with a nicely turned soft **'C'** for the entire rail with a bit more of an incline on the top rail. This is an average all round rail which will work in most conditions.

Using the wooden callipers carefully measure the entire depth of the rail by centimetre from the middle to the tail and then do the same from the middle section through to the nose.

For a manual test, take the board off the trestles and hold it in the classic walking position with the board at your side, your arm around the board in the middle and your hand around the rail. You can feel if the rails are comfortable in your hand as you hold the board.

Finally, clean up and round off the rails using gauze or dragon cloth. The blank at this stage is very fragile and must be handled with maximum care. Avoid unnecessary handling. Use slimline, disposable latex gloves.

For the leash plug, lay the board down on the trestles, deck facing up and use your pencil to mark the leash plug position. Ideally positioned four fingers away from the tail end going up the board, just to the right of the stringer.

Flip the board over and lightly indicate in pencil the position for the fins on the bottom of the board. Take cognisance of the discussion on fins in the previous chapters to decide where you want your fins to be placed.

Marking The Fin Positions...

Unless you have a specific reason you will normally set the fins pointing slightly towards the nose. For an average 6'6" board you will set the back fin three and a half inches from the tail up the board.

For the two side fins set the mark at eleven and a half inches from the tail up the board. The back fin goes on the centre stringer. For the two side fins, use the set square and measure from the outer rails in, a distance of 3.0 centimetres either way. The side fins go on these marks.

For a 7'6" board the measurements will be three and seven eighth inches for the back fin from the tail and thirteen and one eighth inches for the side fins from the tail. The distance for the side fins from the outer rails inwards, will be 3.7 centimetres either way.

Using these measurements as an average, you can determine the fin positions for any board size. You can also pencil in the board's dimensions along the stringer for reference.

You now have your custom designed shaped blank that is ready to have a spray design applied to either the deck or the bottom or both. Handle the blank with care and avoid all dust and dirty areas.

Repeat:- Only handle the board wearing latex gloves.

Finger marks will be difficult to get rid of, as you have no more reserve foam to remove off your masterpiece. If you do, you could alter your foiling by removing too much foam in any one area.

To store the board, stand it on its nose as this offers the least amount of contact with a dirty surface for the blank. Prop it in a corner or against the wall in a clean, dirt free and dust free environment.

The Finished Masterpiece...

Preferably store the blank on a wall mounted surfboard rack. Be careful that it doesn't fall over. The blank is very fragile. It takes very little wind to knock it over. Don't allow anyone to handle the board.

It must go for the spray design as soon as possible...

Some Early Morning Glass To Keep You Stoked...!

~ Six ~

As mentioned previously, if you are not an artist and you want to create a masterpiece on your shaped blank then rather hire a reputable artist. Don't try and be a supreme airbrush magician. If the design you want to do is fairly intricate then rather pay good money to an artist to do the artwork for you.

A good spray on a board can look awesome if done professionally and will definitely increase the re-sale value of your board. However, a spray that is badly done will not only make you unhappy with your board, it'll also have an adverse effect on the re-sale value.

Some Interesting Spray Designs...

What we can do here is show you the basics. How to spray a simple design like a deck or bottom spray or rail sprays or even something a little arty.

First of all, the paints you are going to use must all be acrylic paints. Select your colours and only mix with standard thinners when you are ready to use. You need to mix in thinners in order to get the right texture.

Be careful to ensure you secure the lids on the paint tins when not in use otherwise the thinners will evaporate and leave the paint in a lumpy texture. You can throw the paint away if this happens.

Connect up your compressor. Ideally the compressor unit should be stored outside. Use a long extension lead to power the compressor and feed the hose through the window into your spray booth area. The reason for having the compressor outside is because these units traditionally make a lot of noise when the powerful motor kicks in.

Having paint and thinner fumes plus an extremely irritating loud, throbbing motor in your ear makes the spray booth a very uncomfortable place to be in so remove this irritation and store the compressor outside. Make sure you have a good facemask to protect you from the highly toxic paint and thinner fumes.

Your health depends on this.

You will need two spray nozzles. A standard nozzle and a finer nozzle for the more intricate work. It's very important that the artwork is done directly onto the blank. The board still has to go for lamination, which then protects the artwork forever.

Some shapers put the spray design onto the glass fibre once the board has already been laminated. This is not good as the spray will soon start to erode after a few surfs and you'll lose your design. It will also have a negative effect on the board's re-sale value.

Shapers sometimes do this in order to hide defects on the board. For example a crease or a snap will always be covered by a nice spray design.

Good *'cover-up'* jobs sell boards...!

Carefully place the shaped board on the trestles with the side facing up that you intend working on. Use a soft brush to remove dirt and any loose foam dust off the blank. It must be clean. Continue wearing latex gloves to avoid any direct contact with the exposed blank.

Pencil line all the black pin stripes in first. Use the wood gauge to run the pencil accurately down the length of the board by holding the gauge against the rail and slowly running it down. Stand back and view your work.

Make any alterations necessary.

Taping Up The Rails For Pin Stripes...

Tape up all the black pin lines with standard adhesive masking tape. This is a time consuming exercise and requires a lot of patience. Do it properly. Badly sprayed black pin lines are very unsightly.

Take extra care towards the nose and tail areas where the pin lines will need to turn inwards. Make sure you adhere the tape securely to the blank otherwise the paint will bleed under the tape creating shoddy pin lines.

Remember to tape up the stringer.

Connect up the spray gun and blow out the nozzle with air from the compressor. Fill the gun's bowl with some paint and carefully spray all the pin lines. Use even sweeping strokes and maintain the nozzle at a distance of at least six inches away from the blank.

By exerting pressure on the trigger of the spray gun you will be able to control the density and pattern arc of the spray. You can vary this from a fine mist of paint to a more steady flow as required.

Make sure the paint doesn't run. If it does your mix of paint and thinners is too thin. Thicken your mix with more paint or vice versa. The drying period will be about ten minutes.

Remove all the tape and hey presto - you should be left with nice even black pin lines.

Intricate Sprays...

For more intricate design work, use wide masking tape. Tape the area up where you want your design to be on the board and use your pencil to draw the design onto the tape. Use a scalpel or sharp blade to cut the design out.

Use the fine spray nozzle and carefully spray each colour

independently. Wait for each colour to dry before proceeding onto the next colour. Remove the tape as each section is completed and don't forget to blow out the spray gun nozzle when you change paint colours.

Separate The Colours...

For larger designs, use standard 80gram white sheet paper. This is normally provided from stationers on a roll. You will also need masking tape to secure the paper. Cover the entire design area with the white paper and secure the paper in position with the masking tape.

Take care to ensure that the edges are secured precisely. Pencil in your design on the paper and cut out your design using the scalpel. Once again, spray each colour separately. Remove the paper as each section is completed. Remember to wait for each colour and section to dry before proceeding onto the next one.

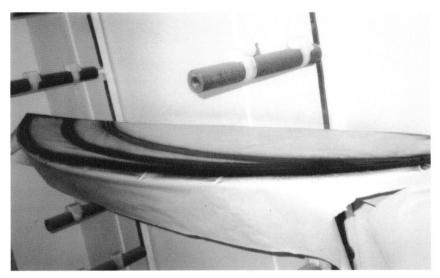

Use Paper Sheets To Cover & Secure With Tape...

This is a time consuming process. The more intricate the design the more elaborate the taping up will be. Use a Duco clear spray to spray over the entire design once completed.

Peel Back The Paper Once the Paint Is Dry...

This will help to stabilize the colours and avoid the design from running when the laminator throws his first coat of resin.

The Finished Spray...

Make sure you clean the spray gun nozzles after every spray. Always store the board out of harm's way once you've completed your design. Preferably, stash the board on a wall mounted surfboard rack.

The board is now going to be laminated.

Yahoo...!

~ Seven ~

This is the lamination stage which is another extreme area. Be sure to wear your face mask as the chemicals you'll be working with are highly toxic. Use rubber gloves to protect your hands and wear a workman's overall.

Place the board with the bottom deck facing up on the trestles. Make sure you have all your materials available. You will need a few plastic trays for your resin and a squeegee plus a wide soft bristle paintbrush.

Placing The Decal...

First up is to place your decal on the board. A decal is the logo or design of your choice that has been silk-screened by a printer onto rice paper. Using rice paper is essential as the resin soaks into the paper making it completely transparent, leaving only the design.

First, dab a bit of resin onto the foam in the position of your choice. This will be the spot where you actually want to have your decal on the board. Now apply the decal over the resin and let it soak through. This will hold the decal in place.

Pull a length of 6oz cloth from the roll of cloth to cover the board from the nose to the tail and cut from the roll using a large pair of sharp scissors. Spread the cloth evenly over the entire length of the board. The cloth must be wider than the board.

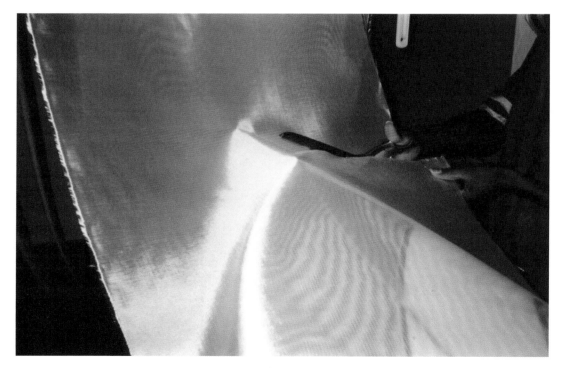

Laying The Cloth...

Leave about a two-inch perimeter of cloth around the board for the overlap and cut all the excess cloth off. To do this, start at the tail of the board and roughly trim off the excess cloth. Ideally, the overlap at the middle of the board can be slightly wider which can then gradually decrease as you get to the nose and similarly towards the tail.

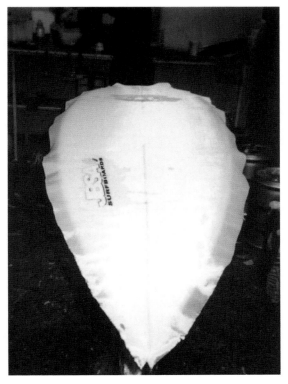

Ensure You leave A Sufficient Perimetre...

The cloth should now adequately cover the foam with an approximate two-inch spare perimeter all the way around the board. Cut in a 'V' on the cloth on both the tail and at the nose tip. This will help the overlaps to fold in easier.

Mix 350ml of laminating resin with 30ml of hardener in one of the plastic trays. Include Styrene in your mix in order to get the required consistency of resin. Otherwise the resin will be too thick and syrupy. This will allow you 10 to 15 minutes working time before the resin starts to get tacky.

Roll the cloth up from the tail to about a third of the way up the board and similarly roll the cloth down from the nose, leaving about a third of the board in the middle area that is still covered with cloth. This will help to prevent the cloth from moving when you apply the squeegee.

Preparation Prior To Lamination...

Pour about a third of the resin that you have mixed onto the exposed cloth on the board. Work quickly but carefully. Use the squeegee to spread the resin evenly.

Unfold the cloth down to the tail and soak with resin. Finish with the nose area by unfolding the cloth and soaking well until the entire bottom deck has been covered. Use the squeegee to mop up all excess resin.

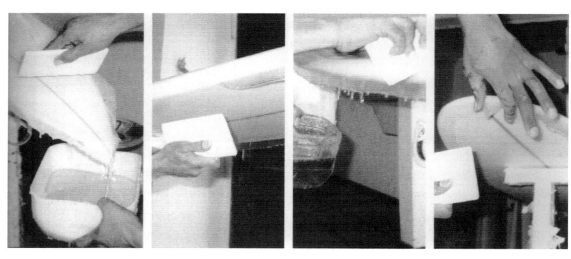

Doing The Overlap...

For the overlap on the rails, fold the two-inch overlap back onto the board and soak with resin. Unfold the overlap back down around the rails with the squeegee and lap onto the foam on the reverse side.

Start at the centre of the rails and work down to the tail and then up towards the nose.

This may take a few attempts but persevere and you will get it right. The bottom should now be completely covered and the glass fibre well soaked with the rails nicely lapped onto the top deck. Remove all air bubbles by using the squeegee with firm strokes from the centre of the board down and then up towards the nose.

Remove all excess resin with the squeegee and use your fingers to remove any threads of glass from the overlap on the rails. Wash up your gloves and squeegee with Acetone.

It is important that you don't leave the board to dry overnight before you do the top deck as the resin will dry at a different rate for both sides. This will result in the resin having a slightly different colour for each side due to the drying process. It will be very evident on the overlaps which are well soaked.

Rather wait until the board is dry and then immediately flip it over. You are going to lay a 4oz and a 6oz layer of cloth on the top deck.

Lay the 4oz cloth over the entire top deck and cut from the roll. Trim all the excess cloth off. Do not allow for any perimeter. Cut the cloth close to the edge of the outer rails all the way around the board with the scissors.

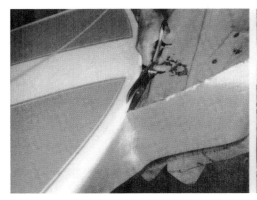

Cut Close For The 4oz & Allow A Perimetre for the 6oz....

Now roll out the 6oz cloth over the 4oz cloth to cover the board. For the perimeter, allow a two-inch overlap so that the 6oz cloth completely covers the 4oz cloth beneath it. This will help in getting the two layers of cloth to overlap properly. Cut all the excess 6oz cloth off with the scissors. Remember to cut a 'V' in the nose and tail areas on the overlap.

Mix a little extra laminating resin and hardener than you did for the bottom deck because you now have two layers of cloth to soak.

As before, roll the cloth up from the tail and the nose towards the middle of the board until only about a third of the middle area of the board is covered with cloth. Pour a third of the resin evenly over the exposed area. Use your squeegee to quickly spread the resin.

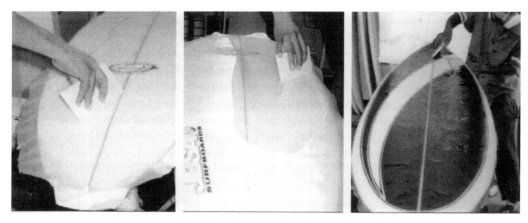

Squeegee The Resin Evenly Over The Cloth...

Unfold the cloth towards the tail and soak with resin. Do the same with the nose area until the entire board has been soaked. Use the squeegee to mop up any excess resin.

Do the rails the same way you did for the bottom deck by first folding back the overlaps and soaking the cloth with resin. Use the squeegee to unfold the overlaps and lap them around the rails onto the bottom deck.

Remove all excess resin with the squeegee by using firm strokes from the centre of the board towards the tail and then up towards the nose. Using your fingers, remove any strands of fibre from the rails. Wash up with Acetone.

You should have a nice even finish on both the bottom and top decks. The overlap area on the rails will be a little rough but that will all be removed with sandpaper later.

Sanding

Wait until the board is completely dry. Use standard masking tape and tape the entire board halfway up along the rails. Imagine that you have split the board in half from rail to rail. This is what the board will resemble once taped up.

Taping The Rails For An Overlap...

Sand-coat resin is a special resin mix that contains Waxol. This is a wax mixed into the resin that automatically rises to the surface of the resin allowing you to easily sandpaper the board without sanding through to the glass fibre.

Many countries refer to this type of resin as Filler Resin, so called because it soaks into everything ensuring a complete seal or waterproofing.

Mix approximately 300ml of sand-coat resin and about 20ml of hardener in a resin tray. Pour some of the resin over the board and use a wide, soft paintbrush to evenly spread the resin. Wet the resin well into the laminate to fill any dry areas of glass.

Use long strokes down the board. Finish off with even strokes across the board and then once again down the board until the entire board has been covered.

Wait until dry. You only need to do the bottom deck once the fins are in position. This sand-coat goes on the top and bottom decks and not the rails hence the tape up.

Once dry, the board will have a slight corduroy or ripple effect on the surface of the resin. This is normal. It is the wax rising to the surface. Check over the board and prick and fill any bubbles that you can find. Wrap 400grit sandpaper onto your hand block and sand finish until smooth.

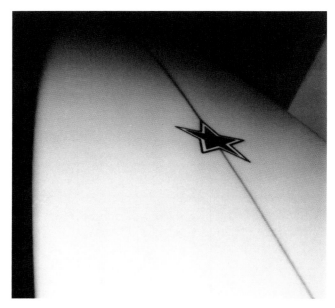

The Sand-Coat...

Fin Placements

Your board is starting to look good. We're going to place the tri-fins. You will have taken note of what we covered in the previous chapters and decided by now what works best for you with regards to fins so you will have already made your marks on the foam when you shaped the blank as to where your fins are going to be placed.

Turn the board over so that the bottom side is face up and place the fins on the pencil markings you originally made. Paint the base of the fins with resin and set them accurately in position. Use masking tape to hold the fins in position. Wait until the resin sets and then remove the tape.

Next, cut out two patches of 4oz cloth for the sides of each fin and one patch for the base of each fin. Unpack the 4oz Roving. Mix 250ml of resin and some hardener in a tray and soak the strip of 4oz Roving and all the patches.

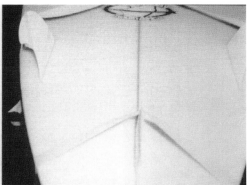

FCS   *Fixed Fin*

Pack the Roving at the base of each fin and cut with the scissors where necessary. Apply the two patches of cloth over the Roving on the side of each fin and the third patch at the base of each fin. The side patches should completely cover the entire fin. Wet resin everything in place and remove all air bubbles with your fingers before the resin starts to set.

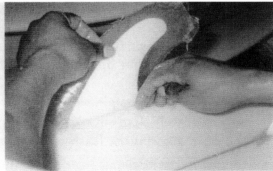

Packing The Bases...

Once the resin on the patches that you've applied to the sides of the fins becomes tacky, use the scissors to trim the excess off the edges of the fins.

Remember, we don't want to have to sandpaper the actual fins too much as the foiling of the fins may be altered so it is important that you accurately trim the excess as close as possible to the perimeter of the fins.

If you've decided to rather opt for a removable fin system like FCS or similar then you need to follow their instruction booklet that is supplied with every installation kit. The booklets are very comprehensive and provide an excellent step-by-step guide.

Now that the fins are in place, you can apply the same sand-coat resin process that you did for the top deck, to the bottom deck. Make sure you first tape up the rails from halfway up.

Leash Plug

Once completed and the bottom deck is dry, turn the board over so that the top deck is face up. We are going to do the leash plug. Make sure you have a standard leash plug available.

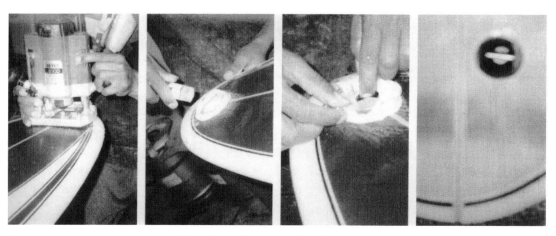

Setting The Leash Plug...

Use a basic Router machine and drill the hole on the deck approximately four fingers from the base of the tail just to the right of the stringer.

Mix white pigment with resin and cut a 4oz piece of glass fibre cloth approximately 4cm square. Insert the cloth patch into the hole and pour in the resin mix. Fit the leash plug and resin in. Sandpaper all the excess resin off and clean up.

Remove all the tape and use the power grinder to remove all resin build-ups, especially around the base of the fins. Use a hard backing pad with 80grit sandpaper over the entire board.

Finish off using the sand-block around the fins and the rails and finally over the bottom and top deck until smooth. Be careful not to over-sand the rails.

Note: Only hand-sand the rails...!

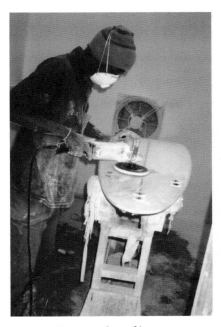

Power Sanding   *Hand Sanding*

On the bottom deck's tail area be careful to leave a sharp edge on the bottom rails at the tail tapering off up both sides of the board. Use the sand-block and 80grit sandpaper for this.

Use 120grit sandpaper to now prepare the board for the finishing coat of resin. Sandpaper the entire board and then clean off with a nice soft brush.

The board should be looking very smooth. Maybe a little dull and lacking in lustre but we'll address that now.

Mix 250ml of finishing or gloss resin using the same mix formulae of resin to hardener. Tape up the board from midway on the rails once again to stop the resin from running onto the bottom deck. Remember to tape up the leash plug so that you don't fill it with resin.

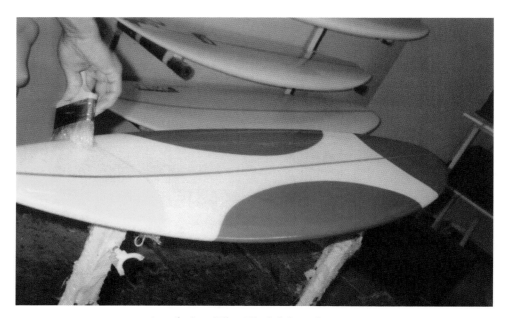

Applying The Finishing Coat...

Finish coat resin is the same resin as sand-coat resin but without Waxol. Laminators often just strain sand-coat resin through a stocking in order to remove all the wax.

Use a soft, wide brush to apply the resin evenly over the deck. Finish off with strokes across the board and finally once again down the board. The brush should just lightly, feather touch the surface of the board.

Also paint the finishing resin on the fins while the deck is face up and the fins are facing down. This will prevent the resin from running off the fins back onto the board.

Wait until dry and then flip the board over and re-tape up the rails. Apply the finish coat as per the top deck using only the weight of the brush up and down the board.

The board is now ready to go through several stages of fine sanding. Sanding takes a lot of effort and patience. You need to sand evenly and be very careful not to over sand through to the foam.

Hand-sand the rails and fins with 180grit paper. Sandpaper the decks with 400grit, 600grit and then 1 200grit paper. To get an even better finish you'll need to go an additional step with water-paper.

Start with 200 dry over the entire board. Progress onto 320 dry and then to 400 dry and finally finish off with 600 wet. Your board at this stage is really starting to look good.

The majority of surfboards will be finished at this stage. Some surfers however opt for a spray finish. This means using a can of *'Protec'* which is a clear acrylic lacquer that is sprayed onto the sanded board to fully seal the fibre glass. You will then need to wet and dry water-paper the board again until smooth and shiny.

For the ultimate finish you can do a high gloss bottom polish. Before you can do this you will need to continue with the water-paper after the 600 wet stage to an 800 wet and then to a 1 000 wet to get the required finish.

Besides looking good, a polished board adds a huge amount of speed to a board especially when surfing down the line, racy reef breaks. This bonus has made this kind of bottom finish very popular.

Apply 1 500 and then 3 000 polish compound to the board. This is actually rubbing compound as used on motor vehicles. Lightly cover the entire board in the compound polish then use your power polisher and high buff the polish until glassy.

Make sure you remove all the excess polish off the board and be careful not to incur any scratches as they will show up. Your board is now looking mirror smooth.

A work of art...!

You will need to leave the board to cure for a few days. Generally, once the smell of the resin has dissipated, indicates the board has sufficiently cured.

The Finished Product

Congratulations!

You have now made your masterpiece. The average lifespan of a surfboard will depend largely on how you look after it. Always keep the board out of direct sun when not in use. This will help to keep your foam a nice white colour. Too much sun will discolour your board a lot quicker than necessary.

Go to a surf-shop and purchase a board bag. This is a bag with padding especially designed for keeping surfboards out of harm's way. Essential for travelling. Don't even think of travelling without a board bag or at the very least a board sock.

While at the surf shop, purchase a good leash. Preferably a reputable brand-name leash because you don't want your leash to snap and have your new board smashed against the rocks.

It does happen...!

Only use *'double swivel'* leashes. This means the leash can turn at both ends preventing the leash from curling up into a mess whilst you are surfing.

If this happens it's a nightmare of note...!

There are a few types of leashes you can get:

First is a thin 5mm leash. Used primarily for competitions and small wave days. Then we have the basic everyday leash which is a 6.5mm leash and finally for big waves you'll want something a little more substantial like an 8.0mm leash. For long boards and Mini-Mals you'll normally use an 8.0mm leash as well but it will be longer.

Finally, while at the surf shop, you will need some wax and maybe a grip. Be careful to purchase the correct wax for the area where you intend to surf. You get cold water wax; cool water wax and warm water wax. These wax formulas have been specifically designed for different water conditions. Use warm water wax in cold conditions and the wax will freeze like glass. You will slip indefinitely.

Grip is always a good purchase, especially a tail grip. It strengthens the tail area and does work as a good tail stop for your back foot when powering a big turn. Using grip across the entire board is not advisable as it will add a lot of weight to your board.

You are now fully prepared to hit the water.

Stoked!

Let's go surfing…

Going For It...!

~ Eight ~

During your surfing career or as a surfboard manufacturer, at some time you are going to be faced with the job of fixing a damaged or dinged board. The topic is vast and varied. Dings come in all shapes and sizes. Damage can be as harsh as a complete snap, where the board snaps in two or as small as a pressure on the deck or a small star on the rail.

For the small dings, you need to clean the ding up with 400grit sandpaper. Paint a clear resin on the area using the normal resin/hardener mix and allow to dry. Water-paper finish the ding until the area is smooth and blends in with the rest of the board.

For a ding that has actually perforated the glass fibre and the foam is exposed, you need to first clean up the area using 400grit sandpaper. If the hole is large, fill it with foam or pour in a mixture of resin and *'Q-Cell'*.

'Q-Cell' is a refined glass fibre dust that once mixed with resin swells up and compresses.

Once you've inserted this mixture into the hole, it will self expand and fill the hole airtight. Cover the area with a patch of 4oz or 6oz cloth and resin over. Sandpaper until smooth. Finally, water-paper finish the area using 600 wet, then 800 wet through to 1 000 wet until a glassy finish is achieved. The ding will be white in colour due to the Q-Cell. This is normal.

The main objective of fixing dings is not just for aesthetic reasons. It is to prevent water from getting to the exposed foam. Water will discolour the foam and add unnecessary weight to the board.

A Basic Snap...

For a complete snap, clean the exposed area with a file and 400grit sandpaper. Strip away the glass fibre that has pulled away from the foam. Strip the glass fibre back until you reach the area where the glass fibre is still firmly secured to the foam. Neatly cut it off using your scalpel. Do this to both pieces of the surfboard and on both top and bottom decks.

Use two or three wooden doweling rods to jam into the centre of the two exposed foam pieces plus some resin and secure the two pieces of the surfboard together with some pressure. Fill all the gaps with *'Q-Cell'* and resin on both sides.

Wait until dry.

Lap the entire break with a layer of 6oz cloth and resin in. Turn the board over and do the same. Sandpaper until smooth using

400grit paper. Water-paper finish the entire area until a nice glassy finish is achieved. Preferably do a nice spray like a *'GT'* stripe or similar, across the snap to hide it.

Covering A Snap With A Spray Design...

The snap area will now be the strongest section of the board. If the board snaps again, it won't snap in the same place. The board will also be a lot heavier due to the repair and obviously won't perform as efficiently as before.

Sell it...!

Keep on Surfing...

Don't Drop In On Locals...!

About The Author - By John *'Zulu'* Smithers

Robin Morris has surfed for more years than he can remember. He lives in paradise – a house on the beach in Jeffreys Bay, awaking each day to gaze down the throat of a magnificent, dancing *Super Tubes*, renowned as the ultimate right hand reef break and rated as one of the top ten perfect breaking waves in the world.

Robin is also an avid musician and is highly respected for his guitar wizardry. His albums have been distributed worldwide via internet music sites like: www.cdbaby.com

He also takes a keen interest in all the arts.

Robin's other books published to-date include:

- Staying Alive – Published By Soldier Of Fortune – USA

- The Marketing Principle – Published By Butterworths – Durban

- Marketing To Townships – Published By Juta – Durban

- Training Your Dog – Published by Media 24 Landbou Weekblad

- Bongeni – Published by Assegai Publishing

- I See Therefore I Am I Think – Published By Assegai Publishing

Robin's CD's include:

- J/Bay On Fire
- One Fine Day
- Jus' Dropping In
- Taking Time
- Best Of Robin Morris
- Orchestral Rock